HERE

I

AM

Diane Zike

Diane Zike

Foolscap & Quill

Cover images courtesy of Darlene Cypser & the
National Aeronautics & Space Administration

ISBN 978-0-9718552-8-1

UPC 803236700085

Published by:
Foolscap & Quill, LLC
P. O. Box 1018
Morrison, CO 80465-1018
www.foolscap-quill.com

Table of Contents

This book is dedicated

to

Father Kinyon

and

Terry

for being

God's presence and love to me

in the darkness and in the light.

And to

my parents

and

my God

who gave me life

and love.

HERE I AM

Introduction

One metaphor for our life story is life as a journey. Yes, mine is and so much more. For me life is also a love story and like my favorite love stories it has a happy ending. It begins and ends with God.

My search has not been to find God or for God to find me; neither of us has been lost although at times I have felt that way. My search is to find God in me. It is a journey that has taken me to the very depths of sanity and it leads me to falling deeper in love with God.

This journey of love requires a willingness to let my Lord lead, not me. I would like to say I am always an obedient Mary, "Here am I, the servant of the Lord; let it be with me according to your word." (Luke 1:38) and a willing Samuel, "Speak, for your servant is listening." (1 Samuel 3:10). Unfortunately I can be a reluctant or angry Jonah; many times I have questioned, and waited, and questioned and waited. Often these times end up with me standing in the middle of the empty church and saying, "Okay, I give up," so God will give me some peace and I can get on with doing his will.

In the poems and prayers and other pieces included here you will find a quiet, shy adolescent who became an idealistic young woman. I struggled through years of depression, and in the midst of it found a calling in pastoral care where my life experiences would serve me well in helping others. My faith journey now leads to writing prayers and meditations as well as poetry.

It may be a struggle to get through the many poems that contain the word "pain." I hope you can make that journey as I believe it is in the pain and the chaos that we can find God. After

1

all God created the world out of darkness and chaos. "The earth was a formless void and darkness covered the face of the deep." (Genesis 1:2)

Now I have chosen to share my writings with the hope that others will find common experiences and bonds. My writing has helped me to express my grief and work through it. A very wise chaplain told me a deep truth many years ago. You cannot go under grief or around it or over it; you have to go through it. This chaplain and another wonderful person were put into my life by God, to tell me God loved me and that God was with me, even when I could not feel that for myself. Now, I hope that light of God's love shines through me so that I might be a blessing to others in the ways that these people were to me.

My journey is about love. I love God with my whole heart and soul and I want to share that love with others. "Here I am, Lord."

Lord, Help me to say "Yes."

Michael Quoist

Poems

My passions
bound to paper

Diane Zike

Coming of Age

I see behind my childhood past.

Diane Zike

I

Why can't I be

what I am

without a need

to know

or search for I?

II

Because without

a questioning

of all that is

and all I am

how can I be?

3/19/1968

Autumn Song

Scarlet ivy drips from branches
Slowly bidding green goodbye;
Falling leaves lap at breezes,
Crumple on the ground and die.

Passers-by don't seem to notice
Fall announcing summer's end,
But some watch signs of seasons changing
And know winter's in the wind.

Skies soon fill with flying flurries
Piling into dunes of white,
And gray, melancholy days
Give way to drowsy, snowed-in nights.

But there is warmth in winter's wind
Knowing spring will come again.

9/23/1968

The music of my life

   played by sad,

      mourning violins

  fills the air

    with sighs.

I cannot escape

   from melodies

   melancholy

    reminding me

      of you.

9/23/1968

Once A Child,
          Too

(to Dawn Marie)

Captured in a photograph
          a child with blowing hair,
sees around a world of wonder;
          looks of childhood linger there.

Staring at the photograph,
          I see behind my childhood past,
and I want to whisper to her,
          "Don't grow old so fast."

There is time for grown-up tears
          and all the lies they tell;
try to stay a little girl
          preserve your childhood well.

I no longer see the world
          through wide and tender eyes,
but I still cling with slipping grasp
          to slipping childhood past.

8/04/1969

My passions

        bound to paper

turn

   slowly

      into ashes;

something less

     than fire,

  trapped

     in words.

2/19/1970

One Downed Daffodil

Their thick, green stems
should stand March's stiff breezes,
holding up a proud face.

Yet they always lean
at precarious angles,
swaying in the breeze.

Are they bowing down
to spring's red royalty,
the mighty emperor tulip?

Such a pretty, sunny face.
Why should they yield
their place in spring?

But one has lost the battle,
fallen flat on its fluted face;
one downed daffodil.

In Flight

Silhouetted by city lights,

arrow-shaped formations

seeking warmer places

cross the night sky.

The night is filled with the voices

of this procession

gossiping,

their patterns shifting and flowing.

Leaders and followers alike

seem confused where they are going

–and so sure

of their destination.

1985

Paths

Our lives

   remind me

of the path

   of a skier's skis.

One swishes softly

   through the snow

      down the mountain side.

The other careens wildly

   through the trees,

      crashing over bumps.

Impossible,

   you say.

I agree.

2/08/1986

14

Emptiness

I sweep away the gathered dust
And find an empty bin.
All I can see is crumbling crust,
There is no bread within.

You offer me an empty cup,
Keep coming back for more.
I know I cannot fill it up;
There's nothing left to pour.

You only come around to take;
You never bring to share.
You never satisfy my ache;
I do not think you care

Some day perhaps you will know
That is why I chose to go.

6/17/1986

The Dark Nights of My Soul

We are healed of grief only when we express it
to the full.

Charles R. Swindoll

Circle of Pain

This is the winter of my pain
ice crystals
that melt anger,
feed anguish.

I am avalanched
by ache
from which I cannot escape.

The chill descends
through raw-rubbed skin
to bone,
to heart.

I am robbed
of strength
by icy waves
of pain.

Life-blood drains,
shattered fragments
of hope
hardened by the chill.

Numb,
Even to the sharp shards
of fear,
life flickers.

I die
inside the pain.
the circle without end
I am trapped within.

1/12/1987

Let Go A Little

Let go a little.

    You can spare a little pain.

   You've worked it

    and worried it;

      now's the time

        to set it free.

Tugging,

   Begging,

     Crying,

You'll always know it's there.

Soon you know

   you'll pick it up

    and clutch it

     to your heart.

cont..

—But for now

let go a little;

you can spare a little pain.

2/20/1987

Spring

You promised me that spring would come.

Tell me, were you lying?

All around the fields are bare;

the daffodils are dying.

How can greening heal the land?

It only hides the scars.

Just the way the clouds blow in

and cover up the stars.

My eyes are glazed to budding life.

I'm gripped by killing chill.

Winter has a hold on me.

Inside I'm frozen still.

Who finds joy in warming sun?

It only follows rain.

Where's the spring inside of me?

I only feel the pain.

3/03/1987

21

I

Your mind brushes
barriers
and recoils
in pain.

You long to lean
but cannot.

So you stand
untouched
and untouching.

Until the pain
without and within
drives you
to seek pain.

Pain.
Pain to feed pain.
Pain to feel pain.
Pain to end pain.

II

You need touch;
fear touching.
You need to hold,
are held
by walls without
walls within.

cont.

To reach out,
to touch
is death.

To live without,
the same.

There is
no safe embrace.

III

In despair
you capitulate.

Wall are welcomed;
pain surrendered to.

Mindless of the agony
you reach out.
Past pain—
to nothingness

Slumping
to your knees
you embrace death.

3/25/87

Touch

I

I retreat
from touch,
from pain,

so far

that I am flesh
turned inside out.

II

I crave
the healing touch;

need hands

to soothe
a scalded soul.

III

Yet touch
I fear,

that needs

to reach
so deep.

cont.

IV

Can loving touch
reach past

the pain

and help
a ravaged heart?

4/06/1987

It is not
just the flesh
that burns
in memory of touch,
when you lie
in the dark
and remember.

It is not
just the mind
that screams,
tortured
by nightmares;
trapped by fear.

The very soul
of you
cries out
in agony;
lies battered,
and bloodied
and dying.

Rape reaches deep
and carves
in body,
mind,
and soul
an endless pit
of unending pain.

4/19/1987

I

In the night
an ominous pair
death and darkness wait.

Tremble, tremble
at their touch.

Your company
they seek.

II

They reach for your hand;
they reach for your heart.
Death and darkness wait.

Tremble, tremble
at their touch.

Your company
they seek.

III

To follow them
is to welcome despair.
Death and darkness wait.

Tremble, tremble
At their touch.

Your company
They seek.

cont.

IV

You reach out
Embracing the pair
Death and darkness await.

Tremble, tremble
At their touch.

Is it their company you seek?

4/19/1987

I

It is the certainty of winter

that I dread;

when all that's living

turns up dead.

And when the breeze of summer

has an icy chill

what is there left

that frost can kill?

II

What can there be

more like living death,

when blood is still

and there is no breath?

When all that once was living

turns up dead,

there is not life;

—the spirit force has fled.

5/23/87

29

Yesterday's Child

The child was clothed

in yesterday's hurt;

it was the only holding

she had.

Wrapped in pain

she slowly died;

it was the only living

she knew.

Trapped in life

she longed for death;

it was the only escape

there was.

5/25/1987

Ascension

How can there be ascension

when rain is coming down?

Living things are battered;

hopes and dreams are drowned

How can there be ascension

when all souls are pressed to earth?

Life-breath is smothered

with no hope of rebirth.

Ascension awaits redemption;

First the sacrifice must die.

Spirits soar in sunshine;

Souls ascend in cloudless sky.

5/29/87

31

I

In pain
I cannot penetrate
the silence

To say
I need a helping hand.

When I stumble
on death's dark road,

I cannot tell
the stepping stone
from sinking sand.

II

You cannot hear
my pleas
for help,

So I reach out
a begging hand.

Help me walk
the stepping stones,

Or I shall perish
in the hell of sinking sand.

6/4/87

One Step Beyond Life

There stands the only love I know,
　　One step beyond life.

He sees my pain—
　　And calls to me,
　　　　And speaks of ending pain.

He reaches out—
　　I long for his embrace
　　To ease the pain.

Love beckons,
　　One step beyond life.

—And I hardly have the strength
　　To hold onto the pain

6/23/1987

33

Memory

Its pain
releases a silent scream
from deep inside
my shattered soul.

Sharp as steel
it slides silently
into my flesh;
drives deep into my mind.

I feel its bite;
know its pain,
but do not
cry out.

Instead,
I glide
on waves of pain
to a place past.

Where I lie
alone
—by memories
buried.

6/23/1987

I

The morning mist
is the shroud
of the dawning day.

Its cold sting
penetrates my flesh.

It settles on my shoulders
like a cloak of pain.

What should be
a world of welcome light,

Is just an echo
of an empty night.

II

Grief such as this
knows no letting in of light.

Shadows are the substance
of my life.

When I look for hope or light
black engulfs again.

I cannot tell dark night
from darker day;

There is no hope
I will find my way.

7/08/87

To Those Who Care

Let me know you hear my pain; that you understand.

Remind me occasionally that I am not the only one who has felt this pain and that it will pass, but do it gently. Remember, right now I feel like my pain is unique and never ending.

Be willing to listen carefully as well as offer words of comfort. I need both.

Have time for me. I need to know you care.

Love me and let me hear and feel your love.

You cannot remind enough of who and what I am, and how much I am loved. I need to hear those words over and over.

Reach out to me. Touch me. Hold me. I need that to show me you care. It confirms your love for me and eases my pain, if only momentarily.

Pray with me and for me. It is with God's help and yours that I will survive.

Going Forward

healing touch
      heavenly grace

Diane Zike

Moment

A brief jet trail
blazes a short, jagged track
across multi-colored, layered clouds
at sunset.

Like a soul which leaves its mark,
a flaming arrow
in a darkening sky,
then it is gone from life—forever.

3/15/1989

I cling

    to silvery threads

        of sanity

    as fragile as angel's wings.

Above an endless starry sky;

    below a bottomless black hole.

I fear the fall

        into despair;

the dark

    of depths unknown.

I seek a place

    of peace

        not pain

where I will feel that I am loved

        at last.

Pray that when my grip slips

    heaven is my destiny.

7/17/1989

AIDS and Death

During my ten years of AIDS ministry there was so much stigma about the disease. A person was abandoned on the lawn of a hospital. I saw a young woman being fed by hospital personnel in a "space suit." Many were forced out of their faith communities. Funerals, if held, were private, with no mention of cause of death in the obituary.

Interfaith AIDS Ministries (IAM) held memorial services for those who died of AIDS. An important part of those services was the reading of the names of those who had died. At the end anyone present could add names. This was often the first, and possibly only, opportunity for many people to acknowledge publicly the death of a loved one.

A man named Cleve Jones had the idea of people making a patchwork quilt, to honor and remember those who had died of AIDS. Out of this loving gesture came a powerful tribute and an amazing work of art, the NAMES Project AIDS Memorial Quilt. The first display was made up of forty panels. A few months later almost 2,000 panels were displayed on the Capitol Mall in Washington, D. C. The quilt, still growing, now contains over 46,000 panels.

I was able to see the quilt in Washington, D. C., and I have also seen parts of it at other displays, conferences and memorial services I have attended. At local displays I took part in the reading of the names. I would often sit together with friends near the panels of people we loved; we would laugh and cry together. It is hard to describe the impact of the quilt. It breaks your heart as you are flooded with the love.

So many people I knew who died: Chris, the president of IAM's board, Phil, a wonderful friend and tireless advocate, and Bill, the first real love of my life. So many gone.... The next poem, "Patchwork Piece," was how I expressed my grief and my love. It is dedicated to all who died and all who care.

Patchwork Piece

I

Individually,

pieces of pain:

a whisper

a word

a hug

a kiss

a touch

a tear

a poem

a prayer

a mother's cry

a final goodbye

pieces of pain

patchwork pieces

cont.

II

Collectively,

    a message to the world:

      love letters

        picture postcards

        family albums

          faithful friends

            shattered dreams

            broken hearts

             "I love you's"

              goodbyes

    patterns of pain

      blankets of love

patchwork peace.

12/1/1990

43

Earthly Bound

(for Ruby)

You've soared to heavenly heights in thoughts,
past clouds and stars and sky.

You've walked with God beyond the earth;
in prayer and praise you fly.

With body bound by earthly needs,
you feel no longer free.

Heaven seems a distant place
you can no longer see.

Look into your heart and know
--so many ways to fly

Yours a spirit born to soar;
there is no limit to your sky.

Not even bounds of gravity
can hold a soul that's free.

3/12/1991

Anointing

I

Sign and seal of holy oil,
gentle touch of hands
upon my head.

Cloak of comfort enveloping,
spreading light and warmth
within my body.

Soothing balm of peace and grace
reaching deep
within my soul.

II

I drink deeply
from this well
of strength.

Healing touch.
Heavenly grace.
Holy Spirit.

III

When again
the darkness threatens,
I seek shield and shelter

In remembrance
of healing touch
heavenly grace
holy presence.

God within.

3/14/1997

45

Indelicate Descent

I

No one saw

the slide

from higher places.

Just

in one stunning instant

the sound of

the descent.

Slipping

sliding

through needles and branches

crashing onto the tree stand

shattering into shards.

II

It was a beautiful ornament;

delicate spun glass.

exquisite in the fragileness,

that was also its demise.

cont.

III

One moment of regret

while picking up the pieces.

If only it had

a gentler landing,

or something

to ease its fall,

it might have survived.

IV

Sharp splintery pieces

all that

remained.

Then swept up.

Gone.

12/26/1998

God

God hears your crying

God hears you

God hears

God knows you hurt

God knows you

God knows

God loves you

God loves

God is there

God is

God

11/19/2000

Here I Am

Out of the golden mists of dawn
my father speaks.

And I,
battling earthly fears
that crowd my mind
can only think,

Here I am.

In the heat of the day
down dusty roads
my Master beckons.

And I,
In weariness
Struggle to my feet
and whisper,

Here I am.

Beyond the jeweled sky
the Spirit calls.

And I,
in wonder
rise toward that sapphire tapestry
and sing into the starry night,

Here I am.

5/03/2001

Homeward Bound

I leave with you a part of me

held by your dying heart.

Take it home.

Remember me.

I walk with you,

prepare for my day, my walk.

And I take with me

that piece you share

of your journey home.

I carry it with me lovingly,

and I will bring it to you.

When, I, too, arrive home.

11/30/2001

Passage

I see before my eyes

    flesh transforming into spirit.

I cannot call you back,

    wanting and not wanting to do so.

I gather you close

    so I can let you go.

Your tomorrows I will no longer know,

    holding onto memories of our yesterdays.

Death is now life for you

    grief for me.

6/1/2002

Death,

    your presence haunted me

      until I was able to turn

        in the darkness

and see the light shining through,

    reducing your dominion

        over me.

6/02/2002

Wings of Straw

They float

    feather-like

        heavy-weighted

   −those straws

landing on your camel-bowed back.

Rise up and fly.

   It is human frailty

      that breaks your spirit.

God gives you wings.

12/6/2004

53

Suicide

It's an exclusive club. As I write these words I realize I am really talking about two exclusive clubs. There is the exclusive club made up of those who commit suicide and the club made up of the survivors. I am a member of the survivors group. You don't know you are until you become one. And you only become a member because someone you loved "joined" the other group.

My ex-husband committed suicide. I went with my son to Henderson, Nevada to claim the body and clean up the apartment. As his mother, I did not want him to go through the terrible ordeal by himself. Also, I felt both my pastoral care training and my emotional distance (through divorce) would enable me to assist him, and help me to get through the process myself. What I found out was that cleaning up a suicide was much messier than I thought in many ways. And my feelings were a lot messier than I expected them to be as well.

Feelings about such a death are hard to describe. I found myself making statements about the suicide to myself, perhaps thinking they would sink in if I said them often enough. They never really have. My mind has questions that can never be answered. Here, anyway.

What I do believe is that God does understand the questions and that God knows the person's pain. And out of his great love and mercy he brings that person home. My child will see his father in heaven some day.

The next two poems, "The Tomb," and "I Want to Turn Time Back," are how I worked through my grief.

The Tomb

Long after the muffled gunshot fades

and the blood-sprayed carpet stiffens,

the body lies

in rigor mortis pose,

the soul

fled

to transfiguration

and redemption.

Except for the blood-spattered wristwatch

counting off the hours

until the mail is opened,

until suspicion and reaction,

the tomb is silent,

awaiting

discovery

desecration

devastation.

2/18/2006

I want to turn time back

I want to turn time back
So you will grow old
gracefully,

I want to turn time back
so you will know your son
and he will have a father.

I want to turn time back
so I can tell you how sorry I am
you came to this sad end.

I want to turn time back
—but I cannot.

I can only let you go,
set us free,
with forgiveness.

I can't turn time back;
I can only say goodbye,
knowing you are welcomed home.

2/26/2006

Here I Am

I answered, 'Here I am, Lord,' and I rose to my feet.

2 Esdras 14:2

Having loved his own who were in the world
he loved them to the end.

John 13: 1

We are his own.

Jesus says so.

He claimed us as his own.

He claimed us as creations of a loving God.

He claimed us by his choice to come into the world.

He claimed us by walking among us, by teaching and healing.

He claimed us by choosing to die for us.

He claimed our sins so we that we could have life eternal.

He claims us when we die by welcoming us home.

He claims us each and every day as children of God.

He claims us out of eternal love for us.

Do we claim him?

2007

59

Drink Deeply of Love

Drink deeply of love;
it comes from the Lord.
It sweetness refreshes our soul.

Jesus gave us the wine,
the fruit of the vine,
that we might taste of his love.

Jesus gave us his blood
to show us his love,
that even a cross could not crush.

When we are drowning in sin
we must turn back to him,
for his precious blood to redeem us.

Jesus again lifts us up
as he offers the cup,
and gives of himself once again.

2007

Maundy Thursday
I
Early April
Maundy Thursday;
snowflakes fly like fireflies.

Mist arises
from the pavement,
pathway to your supper, Lord.

II

I kneel before you,
pour the water;
like my tears it flows.

I am servant;
we are brothers
of the one we love, our Lord.

III

At the table
bread is broken,
bread of life he gives to us.

cont.

Share his cup,
his precious blood;
passion of our loving Lord.

IV

Jesus leaves us
with the promise
of the Spirit and his love.
Time for prayer now
in the garden;
watch one hour with our Lord.

2007

Love

Love

Beyond knowing

Beyond feeling

Beyond imagining

Beyond desiring

Beyond deserving

Beyond dreaming

Beyond wishing

Beyond hope

Beyond possibility

Beyond prayer

Beyond life

Beyond death

Beyond all

But God

2007

Holiness

Holiness is a delicate thing
like heavenly crowns and angels' wings.

Holiness is in grace-filled ways
to honor the Lord with worship and praise.

Holiness is in special things
like prayer books and bibles and hymns that we sing.

Holiness is in the body and bread;
by it our bodies and spirits are fed.

Holiness is in the wine in the cup;
symbol of blood that was offered up.

Holiness comes through anointing and prayer;
blessings and love are everywhere.

Holiness fills our life and our breath
'til God comes to claims us at the hour of death.

Holiness is our Father and Lord
the Holy Spirit and Jesus the Word.

2008

64

For Fr. Bob

*In remembrance of that holy moment
when you raise the consecrated bread up to the heavens
and break the precious body of our Lord.*

My Lord and My God

Holding in my trembling hands
that precious bread,
I gaze upon
my Lord and on my God.

In worship of that body
for me broken,
I kneel before
my Lord, my God, my all.

Enter in my healing Savior,
I adore you.
Precious Jesus,
thou art my Lord
and my God.

1/28/2009

People of God

In our stained-glass shrouded sanctuary we piously pray,

then retreat to pursue our prey in darker corners,

whispering in the bishop's ear,

and to anyone else that will listen.

We attack and dismember the body one by one,

not sparing the head

but making it the primary target.

No one escapes the wrath of the righteous.

We break bread together and then break each other,

proclaiming ourselves holy in word and sign,

inviting outsiders to see our emptiness.

The cleansing of this temple will surely come--

when no one is left to bar the sinners from our doors.

cont.

Among the ruins of broken faith

a church mouse scampers,

seeking any mortal remains.

Father, forgive us.

We, too, are the victims of our own desecration.

Lord, please help us; we will crucify again.

7/26/2009

Jonah, Jonah, Where Would You Be?

Jonah, Jonah,
where would you be
if not for the Lord
and his great mercy?

Tossed overboard
and drowned in the sea,
if not for God's love
that's where you'd be.

Jonah, Jonah
where would you be
if not for the Lord
and his great mercy?

Swallowed by a fish
in the bottom of the sea,
if not for God's love
that's where you'd be.

Jonah, Jonah
where would you be
if not for the Lord
and his great mercy?

The city of Nineveh
would no longer be
if not for the Lord God's
great mercy.

cont.

Jonah, Jonah
where would you be
if not for the Lord
and his great mercy?

Lying in the scorching heat
under a dying tree
if not for God's love
that's where you'd be

Jonah, Jonah
where would you be
if not for the Lord
and his great mercy?

9/19/2011

Looking for God?

Don't search for me in the wandering world;
I know all the ways that you've tried.
You won't find me in material things;
God's love you cannot buy.

Where would you find a loving God?
Where do you think I would be?
If not in the world or things you buy,
Where then could you find me?

Have you looked for me in the places of love,
Have you checked your heart and soul?
You may find my holy presence there,
You won't find silver or gold.

Do you think there's room in your heart for me?
Can you see my love shining through?
I'm really am already there.
And I'll always be close to you.

9/27/2011

Sacred Space

The holy touch of God
His breeze upon my face;
The Spirit dwells within this land,
And in this sacred space.

God's altar is the mountain top
Where eagles soar and dive;
God's creation all around me
Makes me feel so much alive.

I breathe in the scents of spring time blossoms
And hark the summer songbird's trill
I gather painted leaves in fall,

And brace for winter's chill.
Someday I'll leave this planet earth
When Jesus comes for me.
My body will return to dirt;
My spirit will be free.

The world is such a beautiful place
Can heaven be as fair?
I know that where my Lord God is,
My home is with him there.

I think about what heaven's like;
What vision will I see?
I'll gaze upon the face of God
For all eternity!

9/30/2011

Prayers

No one can say his prayers are poor prayers
when he is using the language of love.

John Malliard

Pray Always

Pray all hours.
Pray all days.
Pray at night.
Pray always.

Pray in silence.
Pray out loud.
Pray all alone.
Pray with crowds.

Pray for your family.
Pray for your friends.
Pray for your enemies.
Pray wars will end.

Pray when worried.
Pray when sad.
Pray when happy.
Pray when mad.

Pray to God the Father.
Pray to God the Son.
Pray to God the Spirit.
Pray to the three in one.

Lord Feed Me
Lord Fill me

(Communion Prayer)

Lord Jesus Christ,
please enter my life;
fill my empty heart,
heal my hurting soul.

Lord,
    Feed me
        Fill me
Help me
    Heal me
Lead me
    Love me

Sacred body of Christ,
heavenly bread,
nourish my heart,
feed my soul

Lord,
    Feed me
        Fill me
Help me
    Heal me
Lead me
    Love me

cont.

Precious blood of my Lord,
Spiritual drink,
Soothe my thirsting heart,
Refresh my soul.

Lord,
    Feed me
        Fill me
Help me
    Heal me
Lead me
    Love me

Christ my Redeemer,
Dear Jesus my Lord,
I crave saving grace,
I hunger for love.

Lord,
    Feed me
        Fill me
Help me
    Heal me
Lead me
    Love me

    Amen.

Worthiness

Father God,

I kneel before your awesome presence

and feel my deep unworthiness.

I am a lost sinner,

not worthy of your grace and love.

My child,

My son gave his life for you.

Drink deeply of the grace that he has given you,

and know that you are worthy.

Jesus, Lord,

I thank you for your sacrifice.

Your gift of love

has blessed my life

and made me whole.

cont.

My sister,

Walk with me always;

may the Spirit guide you,

and know that you are worthy.

Loving Spirit,

Thank you for your gracious gifts,

for presence and peace and many blessings.

Lead me in you righteous ways

that I may love always.

Dear one,

You are a child of God.

You are called and claimed.

Know that you are worthy.

Will You?

Wash my feet, Lord?
Will you follow me?

Tonight

Will you let me wash you feet?
Will you follow me?

Wash my feet?
Walk with me.

Tonight

Will you break bread with me?
Will you drink my blood?

Wash my feet?
Walk with me.

Tonight

Will you watch one hour?
Will you pray with me?

Wash my feet?
Walk with me.

Tonight

Will you take my yoke upon you?
Will you bear your cross?

cont.

Wash my feet?
Walk with me.

Tonight

Will you wash my feet?
Follow me

Am I The One?

Lord, is mine the kiss that betrayed you?

Do I betray you in my false gestures of love towards others?

Is mine one of the voices that condemned you?

Do I condemn you through my lies and condemnation of others?

Am I one of the whips that beat you?

Do I beat you with my cruelty towards others?

Is mine one of the mouths that spit on you?

Do I spit on you with the mean things I say?

Am I one of the nails that pierced your hands and feet?

Do I pierce you hands and feet with selfishness and lack of compassion?

Am I the hammer that pounded the nails into your flesh?

Do I hammer others with my pride and arrogance?

Am I the heavy wooden cross you carried?

Do I weigh you down with my sins?

Am I the sword that pierced your dying body?

Do I pierce you with my lack of love?

I am the one.

Forgive me, Lord.

When Words Fail, Jesus

When sorrow burrows
to the very marrow of my bones,
I cry endless tears,
I feel so alone.

When the weight of my worries
drives me to my knees,
can you hear the desperation
in my silent pleas?

When my life is endless night
where I stumble and I fall,
I can't even whisper;
I have no voice to call.

But when words fail, Jesus,
I cling to your cross.
my faith is alive;
hope is not lost.

There is no need for words,
there is no need to call.
You are there, Lord;
you are my all.

Jesus Help Me Carry My Cross

Jesus, sometimes I just need to lean, like a little brother tucked under your arm, hiding in the shadows. I can't face the world right now. I know you understand.

When you were bruised and bloody and beaten, staggering and falling under the weight of the cross, a man helped you carry it for a while. I feel whipped and beaten down right now. I don't know how I will be able to go on. So I am asking, begging, pleading, Jesus help me carry my cross for a little while.

You cried out to your Father in prayer. I cry out to you. Jesus, Lord, have mercy on me.

From the depths of my soul comes the answer:

Come to me little brother, and here take your rest and shelter. From your creation I have always loved you and I will always care for you. I will never abandon you.

I loved you so much I came into the world and lived as you do. I gave my life that you might have life eternal with me. I loved you that much and I always will.

Come here, come to me little brother. Let me wrap my arms around you so you will feel my love. Let me hold you. Let me comfort you. Let me love you.

Yes, I will carry your cross for a while. I have before. I will any time you ask. Come let me love you. Let me give my life for you. All I ask is that you love me in return.

With all my love,

Jesus

God's Work

May all I do be God's work.

May God use all of my being to glorify our Lord's most holy name.

May all I say and do be a reflection of the light and life of Christ.

May I use the mind that God has given me to discern God's will and way.

May I use the ears that God has given me to hear God's word and call.

May I use the mouth that God has given me to speak truth and justice.

May I use the arms that God has given me to embrace God's children.

May I use the feet that God has given me to go where God leads me.

May I use the heart that God has given me to love and be loved.

As I do God's Work

May I do all God's work in Jesus' name.

May I give God the glory for all my work.

May I know that I am blessing and being blessed.

May I feel the Spirit working in me.

84

And when God's work is done

   May I
        Rest
           Relax
               Refresh
                    Renew
                         Reflect
                              Rejoice

With thanks and praise

in the loving arms of the God that created me

and called me to do his work in this world.

Amen.

Thank you, God, for Fathers

Thank you heavenly Father for all the blessings you have given me,

Especially for the Son you gave so willingly.

Thank you for my earthly Dad and all his love for me.

Bless every Father on this earth with health and peace and grace.

Bless all the work that Fathers do so we can be safe and warm.

Watch over our Dads as they guard us to keep us free from harm.

Thank you for kind Fathers' hearts and all their gentleness.

Thank you for Dads' loving arms and all the love they share.

Thank you for the wonderful Dads of children everywhere.

Amen.

Hear the People

People are pleading, Lord,
They are needy and hungry,
I know you will feed them
With your bread of life.

People are shouting, Lord
They are angry and fighting
They want peace and want justice,
Please help that to be.

People are crying, Lord,
They are sick and are dying.
They plead for your mercy
And your healing embrace.

People are praying, Lord,
To you up in heaven,
That you will be with them
In their times of trial.

People are singing, Lord,
Of your love and your grace,
Giving thanks for your blessings
And praise to your name.

Amen.

We Pray for Your Children

Dear God, we pray for all your children, young and old, rich and poor, sick and well, happy and sad; children of all kinds everywhere. We pray for all the children; we pray for ourselves.

Some of us have lost our way or strayed. Please draw us near to you again.

Some of us have been abused by others. Please protect us and heal us.

Some of us and our loved ones have suffered from the effects of natural disasters. Please help us restore our homes and our lives.

Some of us and our loved ones have been victimized by others. Please help us restore our dignity and our lives.

Dear God, we pray for ourselves. We have not cared for your children well.

Many are hungry. Help us feed them

Many are hurting. Help us heal them.

Many are dying. Help us save them.

We need your help and guidance; show us how to care for all your children.

Amen.

All Will Be Well, My Child

Dear God,

What am I going to do?
I loved him and lost him,
And now I'm alone
How am I going to live?

Listen to me.
Listen to me.
All will be well, my child.

Dear God,

What are we going to do?
My husband's been fired,
We just lost our car
And our mortgage is long overdue.

Listen to me.
Listen to me.
All will be well, my child.

Dear God,

What am I going to do?
I can't stop this drinking;
I can't stop this doping.
It's eating me all up inside.

Listen to me.
Listen to me.
All will be well, my child.

cont.

Dear God,

What are we going to do?
We're old and we're sick,
Our money's all gone
And nobody seems to care.

Listen to me.
Listen to me.
All will be well, my child.

Dear God,

What am I going to do?
They tell me I'm dying,
But I never was living,
And now I'm looking to you.

Listen to me.
Listen to me.
All will be well, my child.
All will be well.

Amen.

Thank you, God

Dear God,

Thank you for my life;
Let me live for you.

Thank you for your Son,
Jesus Christ my Lord.

Thank you for your Spirit;
May it be my guide.

Thank you for your word;
May by it I live.

Thank you for your grace;
May it fill my soul.

Thank you for your love;
I will always love you too.

Amen.

Hallowed Be Thy Name

Abba, Father

Holy is your name.

You are in heaven

We are in sin.

Hallowed be thy Name.

Your kingdom come to us

if we follow your will.

Hallowed be thy Name.

You've given us life.

Please give us your life-bread.

Hallowed be thy Name.

Forgive us.

Teach us to forgive.

Hallowed be thy Name.

Save us from all that is evil.

Save us from ourselves.

cont.

Lead us to your love.

Hallowed be thy Name.

You are the Lord of all,

Almighty and most holy,

Praise to you for ever and ever.

Amen.

Hallowed be thy Name.

Hallowed be thy Name.

Care   Fa**T**her

L**O**ve   H**O**ly Spirit

Minister

Com**M**andment   Hear**T**

G**I**ve   **H**ope

Teach   H**E**aling

Co**M**passion

Receive**E**   **L**ight

Lear**N**   W**O**rd

Chris**T**   **R**edeemer

Go**D**

About the Author

Diane Zike has a B. A. in English Literature from the City College of the City University of New York and holds a Master of Arts Degree (Ministry and Culture) from Phillips Theological Seminary in Tulsa, Oklahoma. She received her initial training in pastoral care while assisting in the Tulsa Episcopal Chaplaincy program. Diane completed a unit of Clinical Pastoral Education at Hillcrest Medical Center in Tulsa.

Diane brings a variety of life experiences to the writing of meditations. She was the chaplain and director for Interfaith AIDS Ministries in Tulsa for ten years. Diane served on the Diocesan AIDS Commission of the Episcopal Diocese of Oklahoma. She also worked in hospice and served on a regional advisory board for the Oklahoma Department of Mental Health. Diane has led workshops on hospital visitation, AIDS and death and dying issues and has written brochures and other materials on these topics.

Diane is a member of St. Peter's Episcopal Church in Tulsa, Oklahoma where she provides lay Eucharistic visitation and leads a Wednesday Compline Service.

Diane recently published a book of meditations for Advent through Epiphany: *Annunciation • Incarnation • Manifestation*. She is working on two Lenten meditation books for 2012.

Acknowledgements

Thank you to Darlene A. Cypser for her amazing setup and layout work and for her editing, proofing and promotion. Thanks also for her great patience. My heartfelt thanks to all the people with whom I have shared my poetry over the years

.

Made in the USA
Charleston, SC
22 November 2011